Copyright © 2024 by Yahya Lutfi / Me Youniversity Publishing.

All rights reserved.

This book or any portion thereof may not be reproduced or used in any manner whatsoever without the express written permission of the author or publisher except for the use of brief quotations in a book review.

Disclaimer and Terms of Use:

The Author and Publisher has strived to be as accurate and complete as possible in the creation of this book, notwithstanding the fact that he does not warrant or represent at any time that the contents within are accurate due to the rapidly changing nature of the Internet. While all attempts have been made to verify the information provided in this publication, the Author and Publisher assume no responsibility for errors, omissions, or contrary interpretations of the subject matter herein. Any perceived slights of specific persons, peoples, or organizations are unintentional.

ISBN 978-1-956565-20-1

This book is dedicated to:

My family and many friends in Milwaukee and Minneapolis.

I love you and miss you always.

I know.

I know.

I know.

I know we're looking forward for our trip to Greece this year but...

But I miss Milwaukee.

I'll never see my friend Omar
again or his kids,
or my cousins
Mazie, Melia, Madelyn, Mason,
or my relatives Uncle Mark,
Auntie Kim, or
my cousin Muhammad and
his wife Shaima
in Minneapolis.

Mom I'm so homesick.

Oh why did I plan to go to this faraway place.

Why oh
why oh
why oh

Where everyone talks in Greek.
But they say yasou.

I miss Milwaukee where they have the best cheese and English comes in handy.

Man these were great in Wisconsin and Minneapolis where the people all understand me.

My friend Omar and his kids were nice to me when I watched Adam's World and Jamil and Jamila on my iPad.

In Eau Claire my cousins were friendly to me and even my Uncle Mark and Auntie Kim were nice to me as well.

And I want to be there right now.

Can't wait for a plane.

'cause I'm
homesick,
homesick,
homesick.

If I ever get well,
I'll never leave home again.

My cousin Muhammad hangs out with his sons at his house.

there's a friend named Shaima who's a wife of my cousin Muhammad that I have to see her and her daughters.

Don't have a fever.

But I do feel a pain.

'cause I'm
homesick,
homesick,
homesick.

If I ever get well,
I'll never leave home again.

Man it hurts when you think of your friends at home.

On the state you left behind you.

When you're lost on the other side of the world.

And no one will ever find you

I don't have a fever.

But I do feel a pain

On February 20, 2023, Yahya's mom woke up to find this poem by Yahya.

With their upcoming family trip to Greece, Yahya, who is autistic, was feeling anxious about traveling to a new place. He also missed his family and friends in Milwaukee and Minnesota, whom he hadn't visited in several years due to the pandemic restrictions and aftermath.

Yahya's Homesick Poem expresses his conflicting feelings and nostalgia for his great memories of his family and friends growing up.

Check out Yahya's first book about his adventures!

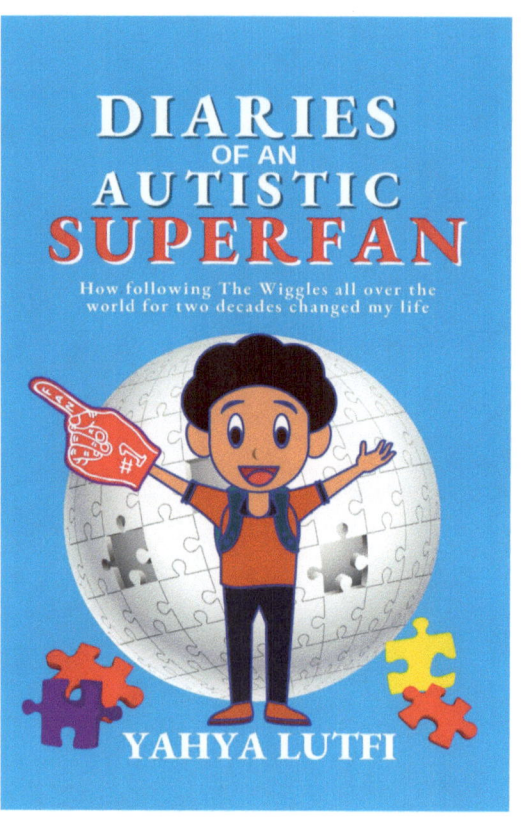

Get the book!

www.ingramcontent.com/pod-product-compliance
Lightning Source LLC
Chambersburg PA
CBHW061400090426
42743CB00002B/89